T0208474

Make It Rain

Increase Your Wealth & Financial Security

VERCIE LARK

BALBOA.
PRESS

A DIVISION OF HAY HOUSE

Balboa Press books may be ordered through booksellers or by contacting:

Balboa Press
A Division of Hay House
1663 Liberty Drive
Bloomington, IN 47403
www.balboapress.com
1 (877) 407-4847

Because of the dynamic nature of the Internet, any web addresses or links contained in
this book may have changed since publication and may no longer be valid. The views
expressed in this work are solely those of the author and do not necessarily reflect the
views of the publisher, and the publisher hereby disclaims any responsibility for them.

The author of this book does not dispense medical advice or prescribe the use
of any technique as a form of treatment for physical, emotional, or medical
problems without the advice of a physician, either directly or indirectly. The
intent of the author is only to offer information of a general nature to help you
in your quest for emotional, spiritual and financial well-being. In the event you
use any of the information in this book for yourself, which is your constitutional
right, the author and the publisher assume no responsibility for your actions.

This book is a work of non-fiction. Unless otherwise noted, the author
and the publisher make no explicit guarantees as to the accuracy of
the information contained in this book and in some cases, names of
people and places have been altered to protect their privacy.

Any people depicted in stock imagery provided by Getty Images are
models, and such images are being used for illustrative purposes only.
Certain stock imagery © Getty Images.

Print information available on the last page.

ISBN: 978-1-9822-0923-0 (sc)
ISBN: 978-1-9822-0921-6 (hc)
ISBN: 978-1-9822-0922-3 (e)

Library of Congress Control Number: 2018909614

Balboa Press rev. date: 08/30/2018

Make It Rain

Learn how to increase the odds you'll **earn** a good living, **accumulate** more wealth, and **discover** the secrets used by successful investors to live well and retire with more financial security.

Contents

Make It Rain

About the Author

Vercie Lark grew up in a family of seven living in west Dayton, Ohio, one of the poorest areas of the city, where he began his journey to one day become a multimillionaire. Vercie graduated from Wilbur Wright High School and attended Central State University before transferring to Wright State University, from which he graduated with an electrical engineering degree in 1986. During college Vercie worked part time as a laborer at Monsanto Research Corporation performing grounds work and inside maintenance until obtaining his first full-time job at Monsanto Research Corporation, making $26,000 a year, which is when he began investing a portion of his earnings for retirement.

Over the past thirty-five years, Vercie and his wife, Lisa, accumulated millions of dollars in personal wealth, starting with initial investments in their respective company retirement plans and later expanding their portfolio of investments to include stocks, bonds, mutual funds, single and multifamily real estate, and small businesses.

Vercie worked for several Fortune 500 companies during his career and, before retiring, led a billion-dollar business providing industry-leading technology and outsourcing services to financial services firms that manage trillions of dollars of wealth for over one hundred million US investors.

Vercie has always had passion for giving and a strong desire to help others fulfill their dreams by volunteering his time, mentoring, and donating portions of his family's wealth to various causes. It is Vercie's passion for giving and his desire to help others improve their financial well-being that led to the creation of *Make It Rain*, a ten-step guide for anyone to follow and create a better life for themselves, their family, and the people in their community. Vercie is living proof that the American dream is still alive, and he hopes that *Make It Rain* helps millions of other Americans earn a better living, accumulate more wealth, and retire financially secure.

Make It Rain

Introduction

Most people born as citizens of the United States or who come to the US from other countries believe in its promise: that anyone who works hard can achieve the American dream, the dream of earning a good living, amassing great wealth, giving back to others, and passing wealth on to their children, grandchildren, and future generations.

The United States economy, like that of many Western societies, thrives based on the principles of capitalism and its people's own self-determination. The more money we earn, the more wealth (capital) we can amass, and the more opportunity we have to secure our financial future and achieve the American dream.

Unfortunately our education system from kindergarten to college focuses on teaching us the skills needed to get a job after graduation. Each of us is left to our own devices to figure out how to increase our wealth through trial and error. Very few people successfully amass great wealth in the United States; those who do are in the top 1 percent and top 10 percent of people in our country. They are the people who figured out how to get rich on their own or who got a lucky break, own businesses, own property, or inherited wealth from their parents.

Since we don't teach people the basics of investing money to build wealth as a graduation requirement in our education system, the vast majority of us miss out on great opportunities to fully utilize the money we earn and eventually achieve our version of the American dream.

The top 1 percent, the wealthiest of Americans, don't work for a living. They live on income produced from their wealth in the form of dividends, long-term capital gains, interest income, rental income, and other sources. The top 10 percent of wealthy Americans are in a similarly pleasing position. They work because they choose to do so. Conversely millions and millions of Americans at the upper, middle, and lower end of the income spectrum end up working throughout their golden years to try to meet their income needs. Many don't invest money in stocks or other assets that generate wealth and provide additional sources of income. Far too many live from paycheck to paycheck, and some live on the verge of financial ruin.

Like millions of Americans, I wasn't born in to a wealthy family. Simply put, I grew up in a low-income community, my parents worked for low wages, and we were poor.

Dissimilar to millions of Americans, from an early age I was determined to become a millionaire. With the support of my wife, family, and close friends, and many others along the way, I achieved my goal. My wife and I took maximum advantage of our primary source of income, the salaries we received from our jobs. We became smarter and smarter investors, we learned from our mistakes, and we were frugal when buying big-ticket items like houses and cars so that we could amass significant wealth over the past thirty years.

It really doesn't take a financial genius to amass more wealth. It does take a little more discipline with your spending, some long-term thinking and patience, the removal of mental barriers to success, learning how to invest wisely, and staying passionate in the pursuit of your financial goals.

There are mounds of financial self-help books, research papers, and articles published each year reporting that Americans on average are not investing enough or saving enough money to last through retirement. Today most researchers and financial investment firms recommend saving seven to ten times your annual income before reaching retirement age. What these people and firms don't do is provide the steps that show us how to save seven to ten times our income, and they rarely provide tips that would help us avoid the common mistakes so many people make with their hard-earned money every day.

Make It Rain is different. In my book, basic investment terms are explained in plain English. You'll get a simple ten-step guide to help you achieve your financial goals while learning the investing secrets (tips) I've gained through lots of trial and error. You'll be a much smarter investor who avoids the painful mistakes that I've made along my journey to secure the financial well-being of me and my family.

You've probably heard the phrase "We learn more from our failures than we learn from our successes." Many authors write books that include exciting stories about their great investment decisions or how they amassed large fortunes overnight. Typically their books include lots of buzzwords (jargon) and pretty charts to convince you to trust their sage advice. They rarely share their investment failures along the way. If in the future you purchase another self-help book from an author who doesn't tell you about good lessons to apply and bad lessons to avoid on the way to success, send it back and get a refund.

I am an engineer by trade; I've always been a tinkerer and problem solver who likes to create systems that help others meet their goals. I've earned a great living creating solutions to help customers, employees, and partners of Fortune 500 companies solve problems and thrive. *Make It Rain* was created to provide a simple solution to help ordinary people earn a better living, amass more wealth, and retire with greater financial security.

As you continue reading, pay close attention to the passages that begin with the phrase "Make It Rain." These passages summarize the key points to remember from each chapter and provide some of the secrets (tips) I've used to make decisions in pursuit of my goals of amassing wealth and securing my family's financial future.

Make It Rain

Chapter 1

Learn New Skills

In this chapter we discuss how education or lack thereof has a positive or negative impact on your lifetime earnings (income) potential, and we discuss various ways to increase your wealth even if you don't have a high school diploma or advanced degree.

Graduating from high school and obtaining a post–high school degree or trade certification is one of the most important factors in determining how much income one earns and how much wealth one accumulates over his or her lifetime.

Step #1	**Establish the goal to obtain a high school diploma or GED, a trade certification, or a college degree.** Graduating from high school or college or earning a trade certification virtually guarantees that you'll find higher-paying jobs and significantly increase your odds of amassing more wealth. Following are examples of educational goals you can use as a reference to help create your own.

Example Goals

- I will graduate from Wilbur Wright High School with a 3.0 GPA as a math major in 2024. I will meet with my teachers weekly to get help with homework assignments and to review mistakes made on quizzes and tests.

- I will graduate from Lincoln Tech as a certified mechanic in 2022 by attending nighttime courses each semester and working as a part-time apprentice for my company to gain hands-on experience starting this year.

- I will graduate from Wright State University with a bachelor degree in engineering and a minor in marketing on May 31, 2022, by completing three to four college courses each semester starting in 2018.

Make it Rain: *The more you learn, the more you earn!* The information shown in Table 1 illustrates how our education level impacts our annual earnings. It is derived from data collected during the 2016 US census on Americans age twenty-five years old or older and contained in a 2017 census report titled "Highest

Educational Levels Reached by Adults in the U.S. Since 1940," dated March 30, 2017.

Education level achieved	Annual earnings
High school diploma	$35,615
Bachelor degree	$65,482
Advanced degree	$92,535
Bachelor degree attained	Annual earnings
Males	$79,927
Females	$50,856

Table 1 - Highest educational levels reached by adjust in the United States since 1940 report.

In addition the report on income and poverty in the United States issued in September 2017 by the United States Census Bureau, indicate the median household income of Americans is $59,039. The chart shown in Figure 1 provides a view of median income based on ethnicity with a range of approximately $39,000 to $81,000 annually.

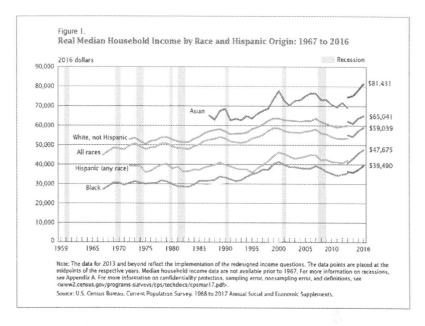

Figure 1.
Real Median Household Income by Race and Hispanic Origin: 1967 to 2016

Figure 1 - 2017 United States census results provided from 2016 survey data.

While there are significant differences in income with regard to demographics such as gender, race, and education level, in all cases the 2016 US census data also overwhelmingly show that regardless of ethnicity you will earn significantly more money each year by educating yourself, completing high school and obtaining a post–high school degree.

Based on my personal observations from managing thousands of people whom I've worked with and on data from the 2016 US census, it's clear that the vast majority of Americans make more than enough money to invest and amass significant wealth while working. What I've also observed is that all of us graduate from high school and college without the skills necessary to successfully acquire wealth or manage our money properly. Our education system lacks specific courses geared to helping us succeed in this critically important aspect of our life. Many high schools and colleges teach the basics of personal finance, household budgeting, writing checks, and balancing a checkbook, and what most view as boring stuff about the economy, accounting, and finance. Unfortunately these classes don't teach us how to invest our money starting with our first job or provide the skills we need to amass greater wealth and live a life free from financial worry. Schools simply help people obtain a job; the rest is up to us to figure out. As a result, many of us are destined to become great spenders (consumers, bargain hunters and coupon clippers) instead of becoming better owners (investors of money), unless we can find someone or something to help us develop the right skills in this area.

The evidence is irrefutably clear: people who graduate high school and get a college degree earn $30,000 to $60,000 more a year than people who drop out. This means that if you're in your twenties or thirties, you could earn an additional one million to two million dollars during your lifetime by simply graduating from high school or college or obtaining a trade certification.

Make It Rain: Two critical steps to complete on your road to riches are graduating from high school and earning a trade certification or college degree. The more you learn, the more you earn! If you haven't graduated from high school or completed college yet, all is not lost. You can always go back and earn a GED or college degree. If you can't go back to school, remember that I wrote *Make It Rain* for anyone who wants to build more wealth, so keep reading. You can find a second job, work overtime in your current job, start a business, invest in real estate, or find other ways to generate more income in order to amass greater wealth and secure your financial future. Your journey will be a little different from others' journey, but it will not be impossible if you're committed and take time to apply the steps outlined in the rest of *Make It Rain*.

Chapter 2

Earn More Money

In this chapter you'll learn the importance of setting goals. You'll develop your own financial goals and begin building the discipline needed to successfully achieve them.

I'll also share a few simple examples of financial goals as a reference to help you create yours.

> **Step #2** **Write down your personal financial goals.** Establish easy-to-remember, realistic goals that allow you to pay yourself first (invest in your future) while paying your monthly expenses on time. Refer to the examples that follow.

Here are a few examples of goals to use as a reference:

Example 1 – Starting at age twenty-five, I will invest $500 per month into my company 401(k) to build a nest egg of at least $200,000 by age sixty-five.

Example 2 – I will accumulate at least $250,000 for retirement by investing $750 per month into an IRA starting at age thirty.

Example 3 – I will double my salary every five years and invest 10 percent of my monthly pay to accumulate $1,000,000 and be able to retire by the age of forty.

The third example above is one of the actual goals I set for myself after graduating from college. Like most people who set a goal, I had no idea how I would actually achieve it, but I believed that by doubling my salary every few years, I would earn enough income to save one million dollars over the course of twenty to twenty-five years. At this early stage of my career, I had zero knowledge of how to invest and create additional means of accumulating wealth.

After a few years of earning more money at my first job out of college I took stock of my bank account and retirement savings and realized that I was not going to achieve my financial goals if I didn't begin to change my spending habits, invest time to learn new skills, look for additional sources of income and find opportunities to increase my pay from work.

Like many working stiffs with a new job after graduating from college I had a lot more discretionary income. Rather than investing more of my income to secure my future I bought a brand new (expensive) Mazda RX7 convertible sports car, spent too much money on non-essential consumer goods like clothes, electronic gadgets, eating out, personal entertainment, vacations, and I'd acquired about $10,000 in credit card debt. I was living a good life but I wasn't secure at all. I like most working stiffs was completely reliant on my work salary alone to support my lifestyle and secure my financial future. After reviewing my wealth at the time I realized that I was not going to achieve my goals and it was time for change. After this realization I made the second most important decision of my life which put me on the right path to become rich and live a life with more financial security. I revised my goals and created table with milestones for increasing my income and overall wealth and wrote them down, actually entered them into a spreadsheet that I updated each month over the past 25 years to track my progress and make adjustments to my investments on my way to achieving my ultimate goal of becoming a millionaire. I also, paid down my credit card debt and began paying it off every month to avoid wasting my hard earned money paying interest and making the credit card company richer.

The table below is an exact copy of the revise goals I set for myself at age 25. As you can see my goals were much clearer and included simple milestones that I needed to achieve forcing me to think of new ways to accumulate well over a million dollars in wealth over the past 25 years and more than double my income (salary) every five years during the course of my career.

Earn A Salary of $100,000 per year before I reach 50	Your Salary Goals
20 Years Old	$20,000
30 Years Old	$40,000
40 Years Old	$80,000
50 Years Old	$100,000

Double Income (Salary) Every 5-10 Years To Invest More For Retirement	My Annual Salary Goals
20 Years Old	$20,000
30 Years Old	$40,000
40 Years Old	$80,000
50 Years Old	$160,000

Double My Networth (Assets minus Liabilities) Every 5-7 Years	My Networth Goals
Year 5	$10,000
Year 10	$20,000
Year 15	$40,000
Year 20	$80,000
Year 25	$160,000
Year 30	$320,000
Year 35	$640,000
Year 40	$1,280,000
Year 45	$2,560,000
Year 50	$5,120,000

By the time I reached age 50 my income was well over $1,000,000 a year and our families overall net worth far and away exceeded the goals I set as a young adult.

Make It Rain: I urge you to develop your own goals or simply use a modified version of the goals I've provided to you based on your current salary and net worth to chart your plan to make it rain! Setting simple goals is a habit that most successful people do to create the vision that they desire and clear milestones to achieve in order to make that vision reality. Set goals to guide you for the rest of your life.

Learn how to earn more money! Throughout my career I've always accepted new jobs (learning opportunities) when they were offered to me. Some of the jobs I accepted included promotions with more pay. Some were lateral jobs with no pay increase, some required me to relocate to new cities, some required me to travel abroad, and some were jobs my colleagues felt were taking a step backward. What I observed along the way is the more opportunities I accepted, especially assignments where others had "failed" and jobs my peers considered too risky "potential career breakers," the more often new opportunities came my way and the more money I made. My career ascent and compensation (salary) surpassed my wildest dreams and surpassed that of the vast majority of those people who played it safe or were unwilling to invest the additional time over the course of their careers to stay relevant as changes occurred in their chosen fields.

To increase the odds of earning higher wages, simply invest in your skills and try new experiences throughout your career to remain marketable as each new decade of societal and technological advancement across countries, industries, and companies ushers in new opportunity for those who are ready. Accept new assignments. Doing these two things led to rapid pay increases and provided much more money to invest each year toward my goal of becoming a millionaire. I've witnessed hundreds of people (family members, friends, and work colleagues) who've decided to forgo investing in their education or professional skills or rejected training and new job opportunities when offered. Some have literally worked for decades, continually passing up new job opportunities and training, only to be laid off or fired with no relevant skills to find a good-paying job while waiting for what they believed was their "perfect job." Many were trapped and desperately hoping they could somehow hold on to their current job until reaching retirement age to draw a pension.

Upon reflection, from my first full-time job, making $26,500 a year, to my last role at DST Systems, where I made over $2,000,000 annually, I have doubled my salary every five to seven years because I committed to do it and I committed to continually invest in my skills and abilities so I would be considered for higher-paying job opportunities. I committed to lifelong learning and always accepted new jobs or volunteer opportunities to hone my skills, broaden my professional experiences, and expand the network of people who could provide me with sound advice when needed.

Make It Rain: It's very rare that we receive a new assignment or job opportunity that perfectly matches our personal and professional career desires. The more we reject new assignments or job opportunities, the more our managers or work colleagues build a perception that we're not really interested in doing what it takes to pursue our dreams or willing to make small sacrifices for the good of the firm. Succeeding in any endeavor often requires us to do something different from what we currently are doing. Take a risk and do something a little different than what others think you should do, and you will change your life forever. The more you learn, the more you earn!

After establishing your financial goals, you'll need to remove the mental hurdles (head trash) that prevent most people from succeeding in achieving their dreams. Many successful people, including professional athletes, entertainers, business leaders, and wealthy people, start or end their days by reading their goals out loud and visualizing the future they desire for themselves and their family. Setting goals is the easy part. Achieving your goals requires getting your mind prepared every day and committing to doing something different—one or two little things within your power—to change your life.

Read the following tips in boldface out loud to begin removing the mental barriers (head trash) that prevent success. Reading aloud will feel weird at first, but if you do it each day, you will begin to get comfortable and start to embrace the statements as your own.

Tip #1 – I am accountable for securing my financial future. I am taking control of my financial future today. Don't believe for one minute that your employer or the government will always be there to help pay for your future retirement and health-care needs. Too many Americans are destitute after working decades for employers and government agencies who have failed them. Blaming the government, employers, friends, or family for one's bad decisions will never put any food on the table or pay the bills.

Tip #2 – I have big dreams, and I will take small steps every day to fulfill them for myself and my family. Most people have big financial dreams but never develop and execute an easy plan (one that entails taking small steps) or learn the skills needed to achieve them. A dream alone is useless without a plan and supporting action.

Tip #3 – I will avoid get-rich-quick schemes and will save a portion of my money to get me through rainy days. Steer clear of get-rich-quick schemes. Avoid them like the plague! Stop playing the lottery, gambling, and investing in get-rich-quick schemes advertised on TV and the internet. Ninety-nine percent of people who try to get rich quick lose much more money than they win or earn. The odds of winning by investing in get-rich-quick schemes are always stacked against you.

Tip #4 – I will automatically invest 10 to 20 percent of my income each month to amass greater wealth and be financially secure through retirement. People young and old avoid investing because of fear, lack of knowledge, or the decision to delay investing, believing they have plenty of time to accumulate wealth for retirement after reaching middle age. Making these simple mistakes causes so many Americans to miss out on accumulating tens to hundreds of thousands of dollars by the time they reach their forties or fifties. Don't procrastinate; start securing your financial future today.

Make It Rain: Set simple goals and consistently take action to increase your income and wealth. Read the tips provided in this chapter every day for the next thirty days to remove mental barriers and gain control of your financial future. Reading these tips out loud will feel weird at first, but just do it. You'll feel more confident in your ability to take control of your future each time you read them out loud.

> **Step #3** **Learn basic financial investment terms to remove the fear of investing.** We aren't born with the knowledge needed to be smart investors. Our schools don't teach us what we need to know to build wealth and retire financially secure. Don't fall prey to get-rich-quick schemes; the odds of getting rich quick are always stacked against you!

"A fool and his money are soon parted." I've actually fallen prey to a get-rich-quick scheme, and so have millions of others. I learned a difficult investment lesson while I was in my twenties. A family friend pitched a deal to me based on the same deal someone she trusted had shared with her. I assumed she knew much more about investing than I since she was much older, she had a great career working at the nearby air force base, she was smart, and she was also a trusted friend of the family.

She'd met with an "investor" who told her she could turn $5,000 into $25,000 in one year and promised that she would be refunded the $5,000 if the investment didn't work out. She couldn't lose. She told me about the investment opportunity and asked if I wanted to get in on it. I said yes and subsequently wired the funds into a bank account using the instructions she provided. I bet you know where this is going. When I called to check on my investment, there was no answer, just a voice mail message. After days and no return call, I began to panic and started calling frantically, never getting a human to answer the phone.

A few months later I received a letter in the mail from the FBI. I'd been duped! The "company" I'd invested in was a complete fraud. I never recouped my money. It was an embarrassing mistake that cost me a lot of my hard-earned cash. I was young and clearly easy prey for an unscrupulous person to take advantage of. Just like me, people young and old are duped out of their money every year by trusted friends and family members. That was an expensive lesson I learned the hard way.

"Sometimes you just get lucky!" I received some great advice after graduating from college and starting work as a full-time engineer at Monsanto Research Corporation. In 1986 my salary increased from $15,000 to $26,500 a year, and as luck would have it I just happened to be in a conversation with a coworker who was ready to retire earlier than most. I asked him how he'd done it. He said, "I invested in Monsanto's retirement plan for over thirty years. You could be in the same position if you start investing now."

I was a little wiser after losing $5,000 from my first investing experience, so I talked with one of Monsanto's retirement benefits advisors to check it out. With that person's help, I opened a 401(k) account and subsequently invested 10 percent of my pretax income into the high-growth fund and also bought Monsanto stock by way of a payroll deduction. Although I didn't quite understand how it all worked, I got lucky. The advisor told me that Monsanto provided a match of up to 6 percent for their 401(k) plan participants. By investing 10 percent of my pay, I received the match. I left Monsanto about six years later, and I'd accumulated over $25,000 in my 401(k). I'd learned another secret (tip): Take advantage of your company's 401(k) match to accumulate more wealth rapidly.

Over my entire career I've always invested in my company's 401(k) plan, and it's paid off big-time. My wife and I have amassed a significant amount of money for retirement in our 401(k) accounts alone by simply investing regularly since our early twenties.

Fear creates doubt. Knowledge removes fear. To remove doubt or fears about investing, take a little time to learn some important investing terms. Please don't skip ahead. Before reading the rest of *Make It Rain*, learn the investing terms that follow:

Net worth = total assets – total liabilities

Your net worth equals the amount of money (cash) and value of assets (houses, stocks, 401(k) funds,

IRAs, company pension value, insurance cash surrender value, cars, boats, bonds, bank CDs, and value of businesses) you own subtracted from the amount of liabilities or debts (credit card balances, home mortgages, car loans, second mortgages, and other loans) you owe. It is important to understand your net worth because it provides an indication of how well you are doing financially and gives you a view of how your investments are tracking (helping or hurting) toward achieving your financial goals.

Positive Net Worth (Good)

The larger your net worth, the more wealth you're amassing to achieve your personal financial goals. Your goal is to continue increasing your net worth throughout your life so you have sufficient money invested that generates income when needed.

Negative Net Worth (Bad)

If you have a negative net worth, you are spending too much money, and you won't achieve your personal financial goals without increasing your investments, earning more money, or eliminating monthly expenses to lower your spending immediately.

Discretionary expenses are bills you pay and purchases you make each month that can be stopped without causing you to miss eating, sleeping, getting to and from your job, or paying for medical expenses and other basic living expenses. Examples of discretionary expenses include but are not limited to buying a car every few years; shopping for new clothes each month; paying for cable TV, internet access, and streaming audio/video services; smoking; going out to the movies each week; eating out regularly; taking vacations; buying coffee from Starbucks; and making other purchases you can do without.

Nondiscretionary expenses are the bills and expenses that you must pay to cover your basic living needs to live life frugally. Nondiscretionary expenses include paying for housing (reasonable rent or a mortgage), paying for basic transportation needs (bus or minimal car needs), buying basic necessities (food, basic clothing, personal care supplies, home care supplies), and paying your utilities (electric, gas, water, and trash only).

Rule of 72

The rule of 72 is a powerful tool, a formula that helps any investor predict how fast his or her money will double when deciding on the types of products (mutual funds, exchange-traded funds [ETFs], real estate investment trusts [REITs], annuities, target date funds, stocks, and/or bonds) to invest in. You will learn more information on these types of investments and how to use them to help you build wealth in the upcoming chapters.

Invest in the right products starting in your early twenties, and your investments should double every seven to ten years, which means four to five times before you retire. When you're selecting investment products, review the historical return-on-investment performance to predict the number of years required to double your money.

Example: A mutual fund investment generating a 7 percent annual return should double in ten years.

The precise calculation: $72 \div 7 = 10.28$ years

Example: An annuity or fixed-income investment generating a 4 percent annual return will double in approximately eighteen years.

The precise calculation: $72 \div 4 = 18$ years

Example: An ETF investment generating a 12 percent annual return will double in approximately six years.

The precise calculation: $72 \div 12 = 6$ years

> **Step #4** **Create a personal budget (your road map) to successfully manage your money.** If you've never created a budget and need help, refer to the appendix and use the budget template provided as a guide. If you already have a budget, use that and simply modify it as you continue reading *Make It Rain.*

Create an emergency fund to cover big unplanned expenses. Do you know that the vast majority of Americans don't even have a few hundred dollars set aside for emergencies?

When you establish your budget (your road map), you can't assume that everything will go as planned. Your emergency fund will provide money to support your family's basic living needs. I suggest saving six to twelve months' income to pay for any major emergencies that arise.

Following are some common emergency situations that could arise and cause you to use your emergency fund:

a. You could be fired or temporarily laid off from your primary job.

b. You may have to take an extended leave of absence because of family illness or another unforeseen reason.

c. Your primary car will break down or be damaged in a wreck, requiring you to spend a large sum of money to fix or replace it.

d. If you own a home, something will undoubtedly break that requires a large investment. I recommend buying a home warranty to cover high-cost emergency repairs. Home warranties can be purchased to pay for major systems (plumbing, heating, cooling, and electrical) and appliance repairs.

e. A natural disaster (tornado, hurricane, flood, earthquake, or fire) could cause you to be homeless and in need of money to pay for living expenses until insurance coverage begins.

Make It Rain: Automatically deposit money into an emergency savings account. Work with your bank or credit union to set up automatic deposits to build your emergency fund. Automatically save for a rainy day.

Next, collect your monthly bills and create a budget (a road map). Make a copy of the budget template located in the appendix, use your own budget to get started and to update, or create a budget from scratch. Enter your monthly income and your monthly expenses from all sources into your budget. Once you've updated the rows completely, add up your expenses and subtract the total from your monthly income to calculate your net income.

Write your net income (positive or negative) in the row at the very bottom left of the worksheet if you're using my budget template.

If your monthly income exceeds your monthly expenses, then you will have a positive net income. Great job! You are living within your means and are already off to a good start financially. If you have a large amount of money left over each month, you should consider investing more of it to build wealth faster and increase your long-term financial security.

Reward yourself and your family for sticking to your budget.

    a. Being disciplined enough to stick to your budget and live within your means is the most difficult decision that you'll make, so rewarding yourself is okay every so often.

    b. Budget money to reward yourself and your family each month or every few months as you see your fortune begin to rise.

    c. Take in a movie, go out for ice cream, order pizza, have weekend family game nights at home, or agree to save up for a weekend getaway to celebrate your progress and have everyone share in the success.

If your monthly expenses exceed your take-home pay, then your net income will be negative. A negative net income means you are living beyond your means, but you likely already knew that. I recommend the following actions if you are living beyond your means:

a. Decide what to eliminate from your discretionary expenses, and potentially adjust your lifestyle to reduce nondiscretionary expenses.

b. Once you decide what to eliminate, stick to your budget.

c. Changing your spending habits will take courage on your part to say no to purchases of things that are not necessary. It takes thirty to sixty days to build new habits. If you really want to make it rain and become more financially secure, or if you want to become a millionaire, it's time to adjust your lifestyle.

d. Meet immediately with your family and agree on the expenses you'll stop so that you can begin living on what you can afford and invest more money to secure your family's financial future.

Make It Rain: Learn the financial terms in this chapter and complete your own budget by referring to the budget template located in the appendix. Spend only what you can afford so you always have sufficient money to invest in yourself (your financial future) before spending money to pay your monthly bills. If you are overspending, re-create your budget and take the next thirty to sixty days to establish habits that will allow you to invest first and reduce your expenses. Create an emergency fund with six to twelve months of income saved up to help you through those rainy days that can wreak havoc in your life.

Chapter 3

Accumulate Wealth

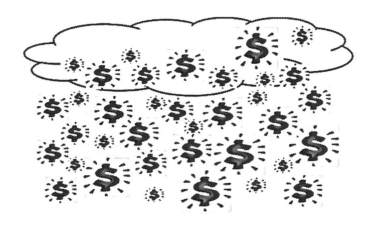

Several important concepts are covered in this chapter to guide you when setting up banking and investment accounts so your wealth begins to grow automatically using your company's payroll deduction facilities.

I've included my personal recommendations on the amount (percentage) of monthly income to save and invest, all the while ensuring that you can pay your bills on time and maintain a good credit rating.

Finally, you'll learn important information to help you take advantage of "catchup contributions," which allows older Americans to invest more money for retirement tax-free after reaching age fifty.

Complete the remaining steps to establish a very simple way to build more wealth while consistently paying for normal living expenses on time for the rest of your life.

Step #5	Open and invest in a personal savings account. Use your company's payroll deduction to automatically deposit 5 to 10 percent of your take-home pay.

Go to a local bank or credit union, open a savings account, and automatically invest 5 to 10 percent each month. Contact your human resources or payroll department to help you set up automatic deposit so that the money is deposited automatically into your personal savings account with each check you receive.

If you bring home a salary of $25,000 per year, you'll need approximately seven to ten times your salary ($200,000 to $250,000) saved to cover your retirement needs. As your salary increases every year, the amount deposited increases, and consequently so will your accumulated savings.

For me, taking this simple step has added thousands of dollars to my family's wealth since my wife and I married over twenty-seven years ago. We set up automatic deposits of 10 percent of our pay and never touched that money. I recommend that anyone with a job take this step to add tens of thousands or hundreds of thousands of dollars to your wealth over ten, twenty, thirty, or forty years. Your savings is an important part of your overall wealth and provides instant access to cash should you ever need it. As you prepare for retirement, a portion of your savings can be invested to generate additional retirement income if you so choose.

Lastly, the cash in your savings account provides another ready source of emergency money if you ever need to spend a large amount of cash in a pinch.

Step #6 Open a personal checking account. Use automatic deposit and bill pay. feature.

Go to your local bank or credit union and open a personal checking account. Preferably open an interest-bearing checking account if your bank offers one so that you accumulate money from your deposits. Have your human resources or payroll department help you set up automatic deposit so that the money is deposited automatically into your personal checking account with each paycheck.

Make It Rain: As you accumulate more money in your checking account, banks will offer you incentives or privileges including free checking, free check writing, free cashier's checks (eliminating the need to go to Western Union, MoneyGram, or other stores to buy money orders and waste your hard-earn money), free ATM fees, higher interest payments, and concierge services to bypass the general 1-800 numbers when you need help. These privileges are just a few of those available as you accumulate more and more wealth in your savings or checking account. Many people aren't aware of these services because they don't keep enough money in their checking or savings accounts to benefit from them. As you accumulate more money ($5,000, $10,000, or more) in your savings or checking account, meet with your bank representative and ask for the perks and privileges that you deserve for investing more of your hard-earned money with the bank. Take advantage of the privileges offered to "wealthier" people.

Use your checking account to automatically pay monthly bills (expenses). Deposit sufficient money to cover all expenses, and set up automatic bill payments so your bills are consistently paid on time and you create a good credit history. By doing this you'll avoid paying unnecessary late fees or having a bad credit rating that prevents you from purchasing a home, a car, or other large-ticket items in the future.

Step #7	Invest 6 to 10 percent of your pretax pay in your company IRA or 401(k) retirement plan using your company's payroll deduction program.

Contact your company's human resources department, set up a retirement account, and make automatic deposits via payroll deduction.

When you invest in a 401(k) retirement plan, you also have the opportunity to take advantage of your company's 401(k) matching program, if one is offered. A large number of companies match (pay you) one dollar for every dollar you invest, up to 6 percent of your gross pay, toward retirement.

This is a great way to double a significant portion of your annual investment and add significantly more wealth for you to access during retirement. Think of it as a gift of "free money." Your company pays you, and you don't have to work more hours to earn it. This is one of the safest ways to accumulate wealth and not have to work so hard for it. Take advantage of your company's generosity in providing matching funds for 401(k) participants.

Investing 6 to 10 percent of your monthly income into a 401(k) or IRA is the no-brainer way to accumulate hundreds of thousands of dollars for retirement.

Step #8	Open and invest in a traditional IRA or a Roth IRA account if your company doesn't offer a pension plan or 401(k) retirement savings plan.

If your company doesn't offer a retirement plan, visit a financial advisor at a local bank, credit union, insurance provider, or brokerage firm to open an individual retirement account (IRA). Deposit at least 6 to 10 percent of your pay each month.

People who invest in IRAs, company 401(k) accounts, and pension plans get to take advantage of growth in stocks, index funds, mutual funds, and other investment products without having to be financial geniuses. These solutions were designed to help everyday people, people who are not professional investors, meet their wealth-creation and retirement income needs.

Before proceeding to the next step, review the following investment terms to gain a basic understanding of the typical products used by successful investors when working with an advisor or deciding to invest on their own:

Annuities – Investment products typically sold by insurance firms and banks to investors looking for low-risk investments that preserve their wealth but provide a fixed income stream. Typically these investment products deliver returns below those of the broader stock market but are more stable than investing in stocks and other high-risk products.

Most people will need to continue growing their wealth and increasing their annual income after retirement to keep up with inflation and other expenses that occur. As a result, I recommend that you consider investing in annuities as a part of your portfolio after retirement, but never invest all of your money into a single annuity or series of annuities, because they typically do not deliver returns that are on par with the stock market over time. Plus, annuities are sometimes difficult to redeem if needed in an emergency.

Certificates of deposit (CDs) – CDs provide a fixed interest payment at the time of maturity (from a few days to several years). CDs provide an investor with a very low risk of cash loss, but they also provide a very low return as of this writing. Over time, investing in these products has gone out of favor since the returns rise and fall with the interest rates. At the time of this writing, the income interest on CDs is extremely low since the broader interest rate environment is well below 4 percent. When you hear on the local or national news that interest rates are well below the historical average, I suggest you avoid investing in CDs.

Bonds – These are fixed-interest investments issued by local, state, or federal agencies and companies that desire to raise funds for projects or operations. They are generally useful as an investment to pay yourself a fixed income during retirement based on the amount you invest and the time frame invested. The longer the time you invest your money, the higher the "bond yield" or return on your investment will be.

Index fund – This is an investment that is based on changes to various stock markets or the bond market indices. These investments will provide a return that is equivalent to the broader stock market index changes (e.g., Dow Jones Industrial, Standard & Poor's, and NASDAQ).

Mutual funds – Investors' money is pooled to invest in products as a way to invest in many companies or sectors while reducing investor risk and creating steady returns. There are hundreds of mutual funds for investors to choose from based on one's risk appetite and investment goals.

Target date funds – These are mutual funds whose investment risk (mix of investments) changes automatically from more aggressive to more conservative over time based on the date that you pick, which is based on the date you plan to retire.

ETFs – Exchange traded funds invest in a collection of stocks and grow or decline based on following some market sector like energy or technology.

Stocks – These are investments that allow you to own individual shares of specific publicly or privately held companies. Your investment increases or decreases based on a company's past performance and future financial outlook of revenue growth, earnings growth, dividend quality, and other factors.

Once your retirement account (401[k], IRA, or pension) is set up, your advisor will provide forms to transfer (move) money from your bank account or set up payroll deductions to fund your new account. You can also pay by check to fund the initial investments you've selected. Take the following recommended actions to maximize your investment results:

a. **Automatically invest money into your company's 401(k) or in a personal IRA account through payroll deduction.** Ask your company benefits representative or your financial advisor to help you set up direct deposit to fund your 401(k) and IRA accounts.

b. **Reinvest all dividends and interest payments automatically.** By reinvesting your dividends and interest, you are positioned to accumulate significant wealth over the next forty to fifty years.

c. **Review your financial statements periodically.** I recommend that you review your statements for accuracy at least annually and only adjust your investment mix every five to seven years based on your age and changing retirement income needs.

I urge you to adjust your spending habits if this passage reflects your current thinking or financial situation, no matter your age and income level. You're thinking, *I can't afford to invest 6 percent to 10 percent of my money right now! I can barely afford to survive on what I make. I'll have plenty of time later to start saving for retirement.*

If you are thinking like this, you're thinking like millions and millions of working stiffs in the United States who have a dream of retiring but who have decided to avoid actions (making small sacrifices) to make it happen. I've seen so many of my relatives, friends, and work colleagues make this dreadful mistake time and time again, only to end their lives as poor as they were when they started, and often leaving a huge financial burden on their family after they die. Too many of my family members, friends, and coworkers in their sixties and seventies have no choice but to continue working or trying to find work because they decided that saving a little money to secure their futures was something they'd worry about when they "got old." If they had been truly honest with themselves long ago, they would have known they were living paycheck to paycheck and needed to make a simple lifestyle change to meet their financial needs after retirement.

Even if money's really tight right now and you feel like you can barely survive on what you make, have some courage. I urge you to start saving or investing $5, $10, $20, or $50 automatically with your very next paycheck. Every little bit helps to build more wealth regardless of your age, and doing it starts to create the discipline you need to succeed. You'll be amazed at how much money you accumulate by simply investing a very small amount of money with each paycheck over five, ten, twenty, thirty, or forty years. You'll be amazed at how easy it really is to make it rain!

If you're age fifty or older, take advantage of "catchup contributions." Our government allows older Americans to make catchup contributions, that is, to invest more money for retirement, after they reach age fifty. People are living longer, so their wealth needs to last longer than past generations of Americans.

Anyone age fifty or older should consider investing up to the maximum amount allowed by the IRS in catchup contributions. This is one of the secrets (tips) that some Americans appear to be unaware of or lack understanding of. This tax change was provided by our friendly US government to help us accumulate much more wealth over the last ten to fifteen working years leading up to our retirement. Taking advantage of catchup contributions after age fifty will generate hundreds, and in some cases thousands, of dollars in additional income for you after retirement.

I started investing more of my money to take advantage of catchup contributions at age fifty. There's no reason that you shouldn't do the same.

The maximum amount of money that you're allowed to invest as a catchup contribution has increased significantly from 2015 to 2018. To be sure you take full advantage of this gift from the government, I recommend talking with your company's retirement plan representative or IRA plan provider to obtain the most current information.

Make It Rain: The vast majority of Americans have not invested sufficiently to support their retirement needs. If you happen to be one of these people, start by investing a small amount ($5, $10, $20, $50, or $100) equivalent to the cost of a trip to the movies, a concert, a few Starbucks or Dunkin' Donut coffees, or the cost of eating fast food a few times each week to accumulate more wealth. For those who are fifty years of age or older, I strongly recommend taking advantage of catchup contributions to accumulate much more wealth at a faster rate before your big retirement party happens.

Reduce your asset allocation risk (investment risk) as you age. As you age, you should begin shifting more of your investments into assets that are less risky, that is, have less potential of losing money, especially if you are seven to ten years away from retiring.

Specifically, as you reach the ages of forty and fifty, meet with a financial advisor or take action to reallocate your investments so that larger and larger portions of your accumulated wealth are invested in low- to moderate-risk products, versus high-flying stocks or other high-risk investments. Reallocating (adjusting) your risk will ensure that you continue to build wealth while protecting your investments from big losses. And it will provide a retirement income stream to cover your needs as inflation and the cost of living rises.

Most retirement plan providers have simple solutions (investment products) you can use to automatically adjust your asset allocation mix of investments in stocks, bonds, mutual funds, and other assets and reduce risk as you age.

Talk with your company retirement plan representative or talk with a financial advisor to communicate your investment goals and the date that you plan to retire. This person will create a target date program or similar plan and put it on autopilot so that you can relax—set it and forget it so to speak. Should your financial goals or target retirement date change, simply meet again with your advisor to discuss the changes, and he or she will readjust your mix of investments to increase the odds of meeting your new financial goals.

Make It Rain: Start investing in your company pension plan, 401(k), or IRA as soon as possible. Automatically invest through your company's payroll deduction program to amass significant wealth for you and your family during good and bad times. If you are age fifty or older, take advantage of catchup contributions, if you haven't done so already. Lastly, once you reach age forty or fifty, begin adjusting your asset allocation mix (risk) to help preserve your accumulated wealth for retirement and meet other expense needs that could arise.

The next chart shows the actual results from one of my retirement accounts. While your results will vary from mine, I felt it important to share real results in order to reinforce that anyone can "make it rain" no matter where they start out in life. I began investing in this account when I started my first job, working at Monsanto, over thirty years ago.

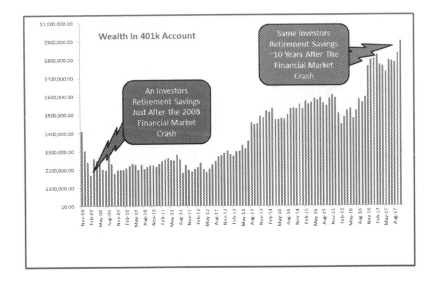

From 2007 to 2009 our 401(k) investments fell sharply as a result of the financial (banking) market crash. I didn't panic. I was not planning to retire within the next five to ten years. I relaxed, confident that sooner or later the markets would rise and my wife and I would make out like bandits. As you can also see from the foregoing chart our investment in this particular account doubled in the last ten years.

Make It Rain: Never succumb to fear when the markets crash. These are buying opportunities.

When I was younger, there were a few times I succumbed to fear and sold my investment positions to "preserve" my wealth when the financial markets crashed. Instead of letting my investments ride, I sold my investments and waited until I was confident that the stock market was on the upswing before I put my money back to work. I have done that a few times in my life and as a result missed the beginnings of some of the biggest stock market rallies (recoveries) in US history. Selling during market crashes turned out to be the biggest boneheaded decision I've made over my investing career. Had I not succumbed to fear during those times, my accumulated wealth would be far greater today, as would the value of some of my other investments.

History proves that the financial market always trend upward (increasing in value) over time. I now know that there will be times when the markets crash and I lose some money temporarily, but it's those times that create great opportunities to double down versus succumb to fear. I've learned to invest for the long term and make decisions that I stick with for five, seven, or ten years. I've learned there's no need to chase the latest high-flying stocks, try to pick the best time to invest, or try get-rich-quick schemes.

Make It Rain: Control your emotions and patiently invest for the long term to accumulate greater wealth. There will always be market ups and downs. Don't panic when the markets drop. The hardest thing to do is to keep your emotions in check when you see your wealth drop like a rock. Stick to your investment plan, knowing full well the financial markets always recover and you'll make out like a bandit if you're patient. Don't try to figure out the best time to start investing. Just start with your next paycheck, invest consistently (regularly) for the rest of your life, and make it rain!

Step #9	Purchase your first home or a vacation home that you can afford.

Buying a home is one of the most common ways that people build wealth in the United States. If you are interested in buying a home, it's important to buy the house you need versus the house you can afford. Many times your banker, credit union loan officer, and realtor will assess your income, credit history, and wealth to prequalify you to let you know what your maximum loan amount could be. They may offer to include all kinds of costs into the mortgage to lower out-of-pocket expenses by saying, "It will only add a few dollars to your monthly mortgage payment."

Your friendly lender and realtor are trying to get you to spend more money so that they may line their pockets with your hard-earned cash. When you fall for this sales pitch, the banker or mortgage lender gets thousands of dollars more in interest from you over the life of the loan, your friendly realtor receives a much higher commission check from you, and the closing (title) company will receive more fees for processing your loan. Everyone wins except you!

Make It Rain: "We've never been house-poor, and neither should you be." My wife and I have never been house-poor, unable to cover our living needs, or unable to have fun because we decided to overextend ourselves by purchasing a big fancy new house or one that was way too expensive.

We've always looked for and purchased homes that were right around the average market price in decent neighborhoods and at prices that were well under what we could afford. We've historically invested no more than 25 percent of our take-home pay to cover our mortgage and insurance, versus spending the "recommended" 30 percent of our gross pay that realtors and bankers told us we could afford. Before you go house hunting with a realtor, sit down and revise your budget. Set the maximum budget for all home expenses, including the mortgage, insurance, home association dues where applicable, and property taxes. Remember that the mortgage is just one of the new expenses you'll have to cover while continuing to invest regularly to achieve your long-term financial goals.

I strongly recommend that you apply the following tips when deciding what to include in your budget and ultimately purchasing a home or making other real estate investments:

a. **Budget for home maintenance and repairs.** Buying a home will cause you to buy furniture, buy home fixtures, and pay for lots of home repairs. It's important that you buy a home that you can comfortably afford while also paying property taxes, homeowner association fees, monthly utilities, property insurance, and maintenance costs on time.

b. **Go to your local bank, credit union, or mortgage company and get preapproved.** Before you go shopping for a home, contact a few lenders and apply for a home loan to find out what your maximum loan amount could be. Make sure you compare interest rates, payment terms, closing costs, and early termination fees, and select the lender who offers you the best deal. After selecting a lender with the best terms, update your budget to ensure that you can afford the monthly payments.

c. **Buy a home that is priced below the maximum loan amount.** Never buy a home based on the monthly payment your lender or realtor thinks you can afford. Ideally you'll buy a home that allows you to cover the monthly mortgage and insurance costs by paying no more than 25 percent of your take-home pay each month.

d. **Buy a home warranty.** When buying a resale home, you will have unforeseen home repairs, so buy a *home warranty* with your purchase to avoid having to dip into your emergency savings or take out a loan to cover big repairs.

e. **Never roll closing costs into your mortgage.** Your lender or realtor may say, "We can lower your down payment and include the closing cost in your mortgage payment. It will only increase your monthly payment by twenty-five or fifty bucks." Don't fall for this one. If you agree, you will end up paying thousands of dollars in additional interest charges over the term (fifteen, twenty, or thirty years) of your mortgage. Including closing costs in the loan amount is never a good idea in my opinion. If you can't afford to pay the closing cost out of your own pocket, find a cheaper house or wait until you've saved enough money to be able to do so.

f. **Never take a loan against your retirement plan (401[k]) to pay for a house, school tuition, or other big purchases.** I've never done this personally, but I know people who have. They want a big, beautiful house or think they owe it to their kids to pay their college tuition and take a loan against their 401(k). Once you take a loan on your 401(k), the money you repay goes toward repaying the loan, and if you don't pay the loan back in time, it is treated as income and will be taxed. If you can't afford to save enough money for the house or pay for college without tapping into your 401(k), find a cheaper house to buy or a cheaper college for your child to attend.

Following are some real-life examples from my own experiences to help guide your financial decisions when purchasing residential real estate in the future:

My first home cost $22,000, and as luck would have it I rented two of the three bedrooms to family members. Their rent payments covered the mortgage, and we all split the utilities. I learned a great lesson by way of pure luck. I learned that buying and renting real estate was a good way to increase my income. I was living almost rent-free and accumulating wealth because of this one decision to rent out the rooms I wasn't using after buying my first house.

I purchased my second home after moving to Houston, Texas, in 1989 for approximately $75,000 while making a salary of about $33,000 annually. I can tell you that I was really nervous about this big investment since it was the largest one of my life and no one in my immediate family had ever purchased a house near this price. I could have purchased a house that cost $100,000 at the time based on my income, but I stuck to my plan and purchased a home that was well below my maximum loan amount. I purchased a home warranty with this home because it was about thirty years old at the time.

My wife and I continue to use the same approach for all of our purchases to ensure we never end up house-poor.

Buying a home and investing in real estate is very exciting and stressful at the same time. Keep your wits about you! What matters most is not how much you pay (spend) for your home or investment property. What matters most is that you buy what you need, don't become house-poor, and keep investing more of your money, versus tying it up in home loans or by making expensive purchases of things to fill the rooms of a big house.

While I didn't go into a lot of detail about my experiences related to managing investment property as a way to create more income and accumulate wealth, I recommend you consider it as an option after taking the other investment recommendations outlined in my book.

Make It Rain: Buy the family home or vacation property that you can easily afford. Always remember that you have to pay the mortgage after the seller, realtor, title company, and loan officer have made their money. I recommend investing no more than 25 percent of your monthly take-home pay to cover your mortgage, homeowners insurance, property taxes, and routine home repairs. Buying a home can be a great investment if you don't overextend your budget to pay for it and negatively impact your ability to sufficiently invest to secure your financial future. Happy house hunting!

Chapter 4

Discover the Secrets

In this chapter I provide some secrets (tips) I've used for you to consider when deciding how to handle big events over the course of your life.

Life happens! If it can happen, it will happen! There are all sorts of significant life events that occur, including getting married, buying a car, buying a house, having children, sending kids to college, losing a job, having an extended illness, or experiencing the passing of a spouse. Rather than let life happen to you, plan ahead for the things that happen to most everyone you know.

Life Event #1 – You're Getting
Married to Someone Special!

There's nothing better to motivate you than finding that special person to help you provide the basics (food, shelter, clothing, money, etc.) and raise a family. It is great to support each other as you both fulfill your dreams.

It's critical to get on the same page with your partner before you're married so that there are no financial secrets between you. Many couples fall out of love and get divorced over matters of money or debt or because they've kept financial secrets from each other. You can easily avoid this type of disaster by discussing your financial goals and reviewing each other's personal finances long before getting married to ensure that both of you are on the same page with regard to money matters.

I recommend you do the following once you're engaged to be married or before living together as a couple:

a.   **First, sit down with your partner and review each other's finances.** Discuss the decisions you've made to secure your financial future (investment in savings, retirement, real estate, stocks, and bonds, emergency fund, personal debts, savings accounts, secured loans, etc.). Build your budget together to figure out how you will cover all the expenses before and after the wedding, even if one parent or the other is footing the bill. It's important for you to figure out how you will get along after the wedding is over. It's also important for the two of you to know what your collective financial game plan is and invest enough money for the future while also paying monthly bills on time.

b. **Second, discuss your wedding budget and your estimated monthly expense needs after the wedding.** Here's a tip: If you aren't already married, save up for the wedding and live as if you're already married financially. If you are able to live on less and save more money before you're married, you already have enough income to cover your needs, so keep saving the same amount after the wedding is over. Taking this simple action provides an easy way to begin building wealth together.

c. **Third, increase your retirement savings (401[k] and/or IRA) automatic payroll deduction.** You'll likely pay less income tax after you're married if you are able to file a joint tax return. Invest more into your 401(k) or IRA, or just save more to generate additional wealth to secure your future. You've been living without the money that was previously being paid to the IRS, so just sock it away and make it rain!

A valuable lesson based on my own experience with getting married: Lisa and I have been married for over twenty-five years. When we decided to get married, we sat down and did the typical things that many Americans do. We started to plan our wedding. We spent a little time thinking about the wedding and inviting lots of family members and friends to be with us for this special event.

I have a very large family, and so does she. After reviewing the wedding list, understanding how much money we would need to spend to have a wedding and reception, we decided to have our wedding in Houston at the justice of the peace and then travel to Ohio to have a reception with friends and family. We saved a lot of money and got to spend quality time with the people who really mattered in our lives, versus putting on a big show for others.

I am not recommending that you do what we did when you decide to get married, but I wanted to share the story to convey the idea that it's okay to do things that others won't. It's okay not to try to keep up with the Joneses. Those early decisions that my wife and I made set us on a great course and helped secure our financial future. We all have choices to make. Don't get too caught up in making everyone else happy. They likely won't be there when/if you need money or fall on hard times.

Make It Rain: Review your financial situation before you're married or moving in together to get on the same page and align your financial goals. Once you're married, think about your future financial needs, revise your budget (road map), and adjust your investments so that both of you are contributing toward your financial future.

Life Event #2 – We're Going To Have a Baby!!

Hopefully it's an exciting time for you and your partner. This is another perfect time to review your finances and adjust your monthly investments to increase the odds that you will have money to cover lots of new expenses, including babysitting, day care, school needs, baby necessities, a new car or van, baby food, diapers, and college-related costs. There's no better time to plan for the future than the time before your new bundle of joy arrives.

You should establish a new budget during your or your spouse's first trimester and plan to set up a college fund for your child soon after the baby arrives if you expect to help pay his or her college expenses.

You'll need to increase your nondiscretionary expense budget before the baby arrives to cover additional health insurance premiums and so forth. Talk with a few friends who've had a child recently to get a good idea of the expenses involved, and add these expenses to your personal budget.

Make It Rain: This is not a time to try to keep up with the Joneses. If you live within your means, you'll be happier, your family will be significantly less stressed, and you will have more money to enjoy time with your new baby after he or she arrives.

Below are some items to consider as you plan for the additional expenses or potential income loss that could occur before or after your child's birth:

a. **Review your expenses and update your budget** to include an estimate of all increased and new expenses necessary to support the addition(s) to the family.

b. **Decide what type of school (public or private)** that your child will attend from early childhood, for kindergarten, and through to high school in order to estimate the expenses that you need to cover for day care.

c. **Decide how much money you want to contribute to your child's college tuition** and set up a college fund immediately after the baby arrives. If necessary, contact a financial advisor or banker to help you decide how to invest in your state's tax-free 529 College Choice plan or a trust fund for your child. Many states have different rules to follow to gain the tax advantage of investing in a trust for college. To ensure you make the best decision in this area, I strongly recommend that you consult with a financial advisor who specializes in setting up children's trusts or college funds in your state.

d. **Increase the amount of money in your emergency fund** to cover unexpected things that may arise once the new bundle of joy comes home.

e. **Increase your budget to include expenses for new necessities** including furniture, clothes, toys, food, medicine, activities (birthdays, holidays), trips, and so forth. Budget for necessities, and avoid buying lots of expensive furniture, clothing, or other items that will end up being sold later for pennies on the dollar or go unused.

f. **Reduce your monthly living expenses** during your or your spouse's second trimester to get used to living on less income and to build the discipline needed should you or your spouse have to take off from work for an extended period of time for some unforeseen reason.

g. **Does your company offer paid family medical leave of absence?** If your company or your spouse's company doesn't provide paid family medical leave of absence (FMLA) to cover the birth of a child, you will need to allocate enough money to cover an unexpected loss of income should you or your spouse need to take off from work for an extended period of time. Check with your company human resources representative to confirm the company's FMLA policy relating to treatment during and after childbirth.

A real-life example from my own experience: When my wife and I were expecting our first child, we stopped spending her paycheck in the event she decided to stop working full time. We cut our spending almost in half and lived on my salary at that time. We lived well below our means and saved her income to build up more cash in case we needed it.

After our daughter was born, my wife went back to work and later decided that the stress of work and dealing with day care was not worth it. My wife resigned from her job after three months, and we lived on my salary from that point forward. My income has increased materially since our daughter was born, but that's not the point. The point is that we put our plan in place and curtailed our expenses in case things did not go well after our baby was born. We were prepared to live on less and continued to invest for our family's future.

The next thing we did that helped us prepare for living with a new mouth to feed was not to spend lots of money on lavish toys, baby clothes, and other items that most people buy when they are expecting their first child. My wife and I spent less than $1,000 to outfit our children's room and purchase the basic necessities, whereas many of our friends spent several thousands of dollars on cribs, room makeovers, clothes, and other items that they ended up selling for pennies on the dollar at garage sales. Now I am not suggesting that you do what we did, but I would like you to know that you have choices and that your children really won't care what their bed or room looked like and how much their stroller cost. There's no need to spend more money to try to keep up appearances or keep up with the Joneses.

Make It Rain: Children grow out of everything very fast, including cribs, beds, strollers, car seats, rockers, and other "necessities." Don't fall into the trap of listening to others about what you should or should not buy. Don't go overboard. Be frugal and buy things that are on sale so that you can invest the extra money into your child's college education or a savings account that can be used to pay for additional expenses when it really matters to you and your children.

Life Event #3 – My Car Won't Start.
I'm Late for Work Again!

Your primary car just broke down again! You need a reliable car or van to transport your family to and fro.

Finding an affordable car (new or used) that meets your personal transportation needs can be a very stressful experience. This is true before, during, and after the purchase if you haven't done your homework. Following are a few tips to help guide your financial decisions when you need to buy a car in the future:

a. The worst thing you can do when buying any car is to go to a dealership, a family member, or a private seller and begin negotiating a deal without knowing the value of the car (the average retail price in your area, the manufacturer's suggested retail price [MSRP], the average trade-in value in your area, and the car's mechanical condition).

b. You should take time to research your financing options if you are planning to get a car loan to purchase the vehicle. The less you know about the car and your financing options, the more money you stand to lose (pay) each month until the loan is paid in full. The good news is that there are many reputable car buying websites available where you can research the types of vehicles available in your area and that can help you determine the best price to pay.

c. Similar to buying a house, once you own a car you'll have to pay for additional expenses, such as car insurance, gasoline, routine maintenance, minor repairs, new tires, new brakes, car washes, and fluid replacement. Be sure to budget for ongoing car maintenance and typical repairs.

d. Review your monthly budget, update your investments and expenses, and reduce your monthly spending habits if needed to be certain that you can afford to own and maintain your new car.

If you decide to finance your new car, go to your bank or credit union and get preapproved for a loan to help determine just how much money you can afford to pay each month. Be patient and save enough money to make a down payment to cover 10 to 20 percent of the purchase price. Whenever possible, avoid financing (having a car loan) for more than forty-eight months.

Following are a few tips to consider if you decide to finance the purchase of a new or used car:

a. If you have to finance a car for sixty, seventy-two, or eighty-four months, you are trying to buy a car that is way out of your price range.

b. There's no need to spend more for a car than what you can afford. Buy a more affordable car, and never finance more than four years. Invest the money you save by avoiding the expense of more financing costs just to have a more expensive car that you really can't afford. This will allow you to build more wealth much faster than the average Joe.

c. If you happen to have a car loan with a sixty-, seventy-two-, or eighty-four-month term, I urge you to pay it off much sooner so as to stop making the financing company wealthier by spending your hard-earned money on high-interest loans.

Here are a few more secrets (tips) to help you make a good deal when buying a vehicle:

a. If you're not into spending money to have the latest model on the market, you can save a huge amount of money by buying a gently used (certified preowned) car or by buying a new car that's left over (still on the lot) from last year's new car inventory.

b. When buying a used car or dealership demo, always ask to review the most recent Carfax report to ensure that you know how the car was maintained and whether it's been wrecked or damaged by some other type of incident (flood, tornado, fire, or hailstorm). Knowing the facts about the car before you sit down and negotiate the purchase price will help you get a better deal and prevent you from buying a lemon.

c. If you happen to buy a lemon—a car that is damaged without the damage being disclosed to you, or a car that become irreparable soon after purchase—many states have lemon laws to help you recover your money.

d. I recommend purchasing a twelve-, twenty-four-, or thirty-six-month vehicle engine and power train warranty if the dealer doesn't offer it for free when buying a used car. Having a warranty eliminates the risk of paying for very expensive repairs during the first few years of ownership.

Make It Rain: Research cars within your price range using an online car buying site before going to a dealership to discuss the price or financing for any vehicle. Revise your budget and monthly expenses so that you can continue investing for your future while comfortably paying for your new car. Follow these recommendations and you'll be better armed and more confident to go toe to toe with the sales representative and negotiate a good deal.

Lastly, if you can't get the car that you want at a price you can afford, walk away and find a dealer who will work with you.

Make It Rain

Chapter 5

Let's Make It Rain

We have the power within us to forever change our lives and the lives of those around us. *Make It Rain* was written out of my passion to help millions of everyday people keep more of their hard-earned money, invest wisely to accumulate more wealth, and generate enough income to live on and retire worry-free.

I hope *Make It Rain* has inspired you to use the knowledge you've gained and harness the power within you to create a better life, one filled with more abundance, financial security, and prosperity.

Complete step 10 on the following page to memorialize this day, the day you decided to make it rain!

> ## Step #10   Pledge to use your passion and knowledge to make it rain!

I will graduate from _____

in the year _____ with a degree in _____.

I will have amassed _____ dollars when I am _____ years old by investing _____ percent of my pretax income to secure my future and retire by the age of _____.

I will automatically invest _____ in a retirement savings plan (IRA, 401[k], or other pension plan) starting with my first job. I will automatically invest _____ percent of my after-tax income into a personal savings account each month.

I pledge to create my first budget by [enter date] _____ to establish my goals to achieve financial security by creating a personal budget to help me manage my money and guide my financial decisions. (Refer to the budget template located in the appendix and use it as a guide if you need help creating your own.)

I pledge to review my budget, actual expenses, and investments on the [enter date] _____ of each month for the next twelve months to ensure that my investment plan is on track to achieve my goals.

Printed Name: _____

Signature: _____Date: _____

I hope the insights contained in *Make It Rain* inspire you to pursue your dreams of a better life, one filled with abundance, more wealth, and prosperity for you and your family.

Share copies with friends and family to help millions more make it rain!

Make It Rain

Appendix

Budget Template

Sample Budget

(Use as refence only. The Sample is provided to help create your own personal budget)

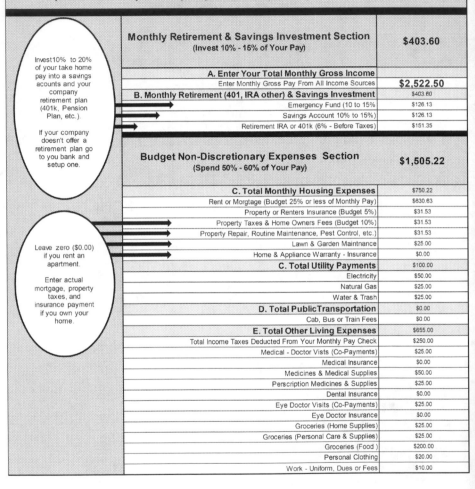

Monthly Retirement & Savings Investment Section (Invest 10% - 15% of Your Pay)	**$403.60**
A. Enter Your Total Monthly Gross Income	
Enter Monthly Gross Pay From All Income Sources	**$2,522.50**
B. Monthly Retirement (401, IRA other) & Savings Investment	$403.60
Emergency Fund (10 to 15%	$126.13
Savings Account 10% to 15%)	$126.13
Retirement IRA or 401k (6% - Before Taxes)	$151.35
Budget Non-Discretionary Expenses Section (Spend 50% - 60% of Your Pay)	**$1,505.22**
C. Total Monthly Housing Expenses	$750.22
Rent or Morgtage (Budget 25% or less of Monthly Pay)	$630.63
Property or Renters Insurance (Budget 5%)	$31.53
Property Taxes & Home Owners Fees (Budget 10%)	$31.53
Property Repair, Routine Maintenance, Pest Control, etc.)	$31.53
Lawn & Garden Maintnance	$25.00
Home & Appliance Warranty - Insurance	$0.00
C. Total Utility Payments	$100.00
Electricity	$50.00
Natural Gas	$25.00
Water & Trash	$25.00
D. Total PublicTransportation	$0.00
Cab, Bus or Train Fees	$0.00
E. Total Other Living Expenses	$655.00
Total Income Taxes Deducted From Your Monthly Pay Check	$250.00
Medical - Doctor Vists (Co-Payments)	$25.00
Medical Insurance	$0.00
Medicines & Medical Supplies	$50.00
Perscription Medicines & Supplies	$25.00
Dental Insurance	$0.00
Eye Doctor Visits (Co-Payments)	$25.00
Eye Doctor Insurance	$0.00
Groceries (Home Supplies)	$25.00
Groceries (Personal Care & Supplies)	$25.00
Groceries (Food)	$200.00
Personal Clothing	$20.00
Work - Uniform, Dues or Fees	$10.00

Invest10% to 20% of your take home pay into a savings acounts and your company retirement plan (401k, Pension Plan, etc.).

If your company doesn't offer a retirement plan go to you bank and setup one.

Leave zero ($0.00) if you rent an apartment.

Enter actual mortgage, property taxes, and insurance payment if you own your home.

Sample Budget
(Use as refence only. The Sample is provided to help create your own personal budget)

Budget Discretionary Expense Budget Section (Spend 10 - 20% of Your Pay)	$862.25

TAKE THE LEAD

If your Estimated Monthly Net Income or your actual monthly Net Income at the bottome of the worksheet is NEGATIVE ($) then you must implement changes to your life style immediatly.

You are living beyond your means and must reduce discretionary expenses or find additional work to increase your take home pay each month.

Reduce your discretionary budget and acutal monthly expenses until your Estimated Net Income is positve by at least $100.00 each month. Doing this will allow you to invest and to secure your financial future.

Item	Amount
F. Total Monthly Expense For Signficant Purchases	$0.00
House Purchase or Down Payment Fund	$0.00
Car Purchase or Down Payment Fund	$0.00
Marriage - Planning A Wedding	$0.00
Birth of a Child - College Fund (529 Plan or UTMA Trust)	$0.00
Life Insurance Policy	$0.00
Other	$0.00
G. Total Monthly Personal Transportation Expenses	$512.25
Car, Van & Motorcycle Payment	$252.25
Gasoline	$100.00
Insurance	$100.00
Car Maintenance & Repairs	$50.00
Car Supplies (Cleaning, Oil/Fluids)	$10.00
Home Storage Rentals	$0.00
H. Total Monthly Family & Personal Entertainment	$50.00
Apartment or Home Furnishings	$0.00
Furniture & Appliance Rentals Fees	$0.00
Phone (Wired or Wireless)	$0.00
Cable TV (ATT, Timewarner, Google, etc.)	$25.00
Internet Access (ATT, TimeWarner, Google, etc.)	$0.00
Streaming TV & Audio Services (Apple, Hulu, Spotify, etc.)	$0.00
Pet Food & Supplies	$0.00
Smoking - Cigarettes, Cigars, Hoka Bars, etc.	$0.00
Drinking - Alcohol, Beer, Wine or Other Libations	$0.00
Eating Out - Lunch or Dinner	$25.00
Evening Out - Movies, Dinner, Dancing, etc.	$0.00
Family Vacation or Weekend GetAWay Fund	$0.00
Holiday & Birthday Gifts (Christmas Fund, etc.)	$0.00
News & Periodical Subscriptions (Newspapers, magazines and Web Sites)	$0.00
I. Total Bank & Credit Cards Payments	$100.00
Prepaid Debit or Phone Cards	$0.00
Visa Credit Card	$100.00
Mastercard Credit Card	$0.00
American Express Credit Card	$0.00
Add Others (Include all Cards)	$0.00
J. Total Department Store Credit Card Payments	$200.00
Walmart	$100.00
Target	$100.00
Home Depot	$0.00
Lowes	$0.00
Macys	$0.00
JC Pennys	$0.00
Gasoline Card	$0.00
Add Others include all Cards)	$0.00
Estimated Monthly Net Income (Calculate your Net income by subtracting sections B through J from A)	($248.57)

95

Printed in the United States
By Bookmasters